BUSY

BUSY

Biblical

TRUTHS

— when —

You Need
a Break

PUBLISHING GROUP

NASHVILLE, TENNESSEE

978-1-5359-1792-6

Published by B&H Publishing Group
Nashville, Tennessee

Dewey Decimal Classification: 242.5
Subject Heading: DEVOTIONAL LITERATURE \
BIBLE—INSPIRATION \ MEDITATIONS \ PRAYERS

1 2 3 4 5 6 7 8 • 22 21 20 19 18

CONTENTS

CONTENTS

Somewhere along the line, the Bible attracted a reputation for being both irrelevant and impossible to understand. Out of touch as well as out of reach. Yet while conclusions like these continue to persist, so does human need for the Bible to be everything God affirms it to be: "living and effective" (Hebrews 4:12), its message "very near you, in your mouth and in your heart" (Deuteronomy 30:14).

If families and friends are to live together in unity . . . if lives are to be whole and fruitful in heart and mind . . . if tragedy and loss and disappointment and confusion are to be survived . . . no, not merely survived but transformed into peace and power and a purposeful way forward . . . you need a Word that is here and now and able to be grasped. You need to "know the truth," because "the truth will set you free" (John 8:32).

That's why you picked up this book. As you are running around, you need to take a step back, sit down, and soak in God's Word.

Filled with Scriptures that speak personally to you this little book is further proof that God intends His Word to share living space with your present reality. Always in touch. Always within reach. No matter where you are, or what you are going through, allow this book to help direct you to the Scriptures you need most.

Anxiety can come up in every part of our lives. Beneath our anxieties is a need to feel in control. Control is impossible, and trying to hold on to it will only leave you scrambling and stressed. Our peace is found in knowing that the Creator of the universe holds us safely in the palm of His hand and will protect us no matter the situation in which we land. Release control to God, and allow yourself to be free in His hand.

"Therefore I tell you: Don't worry about your life, what you will eat or what you will drink; or about your body, what you will wear. Isn't life more than food and the body more than clothing? Consider the birds of the sky: They don't sow or reap or gather into barns, yet your heavenly Father feeds them. Aren't you worth more than they? Can any of you add one moment to his life-span by worrying?"

Matthew 6:25–27

———

Humble yourselves, therefore, under the mighty hand of God, so that he may exalt you at the proper time, casting all your cares on him, because he cares about you.

1 Peter 5:6–7

"Peace I leave with you. My peace I give to you. I do not give to you as the world gives. Don't let your heart be troubled or fearful."

    John 14:27

———

Don't worry about anything, but in everything, through prayer and petition with thanksgiving, present your requests to God. And the peace of God, which surpasses all understanding, will guard your hearts and minds in Christ Jesus.

    Philippians 4:6–7

———

For God has not given us a spirit of fear, but one of power, love, and sound judgment.

    2 Timothy 1:7

Heavenly Father, no matter how much I wish it was not true, there are things that are outside of my control. I worry that I am not doing enough, or too much, or am not fully known or fully loved. I feel lost without some kind of control. Help me to leave my anxieties at Your feet. I entrust to You my anxieties, knowing that Your peace will guard my heart and mind. Amen

Authority plays a part in every area of your life, and you simultaneously have roles on both sides of the equation. At work you have a boss to submit to, while at home you direct your children. At church you are led by your pastor, while you may lead your small group. When we fill our schedules to the brim, both our abilities to lead and submit are put to the test. When you get to this point, do not rely on your own ability; seek wisdom in all your decisions from God, who is ultimately in control of every sphere of your life.

Then he said to them, "Give, then, to Caesar the things that are Caesar's, and to God the things that are God's." When they heard this, they were amazed. So they left him and went away.
Matthew 22:21–22

———

Jesus came near and said to them, "All authority has been given to me in heaven and on earth."
Matthew 28:18

———

Let everyone submit to the governing authorities, since there is no authority except from God, and the authorities that exist are instituted by God.
Romans 13:1

For this reason God highly exalted him and gave him the name that is above every name, so that at the name of Jesus every knee will bow—in heaven and on earth and under the earth—and every tongue will confess that Jesus Christ is Lord, to the glory of God the Father.

Philippians 2:9–11

———

Submit to every human authority because of the Lord, whether to the emperor as the supreme authority or to governors as those sent out by him to punish those who do what is evil and to praise those who do what is good. For it is God's will that you silence the ignorance of foolish people by doing good.

1 Peter 2:13–15

Dear Jesus, I praise You for granting me wisdom and grace to be a mirror of godly authority to others, and I willingly submit to Your authority in all things. Father, give me guidance to know when You have called me to lead, and when You have called me to submit. Create in me a humble heart, that even when I am in a place of authority I never forget that I still ultimately fall under Your headship. Amen

In the midst of chaos, it feels impossible to remember the blessings that God has placed in our lives. But even in the whirlwind, He is there. We can experience deep joy when we take notice of the abundant blessings in our lives and praise and thank the Lord for such bountiful grace, even in the midst of feeling overwhelmed. While running around, remember the provisions that God has given you.

"May the LORD bless you and protect you; may the LORD make his face shine on you and be gracious to you; may the LORD look with favor on you and give you peace."

Numbers 6:24–26

―――――

Indeed, we have all received grace upon grace from his fullness, for the law was given through Moses; grace and truth came through Jesus Christ.

John 1:16–17

―――――

And God is able to make every grace overflow to you, so that in every way, always having everything you need, you may excel in every good work.

2 Corinthians 9:8

Blessed is the God and Father of our Lord Jesus Christ, who has blessed us with every spiritual blessing in the heavens in Christ.

   Ephesians 1:3

———

And my God will supply all your needs according to his riches in glory in Christ Jesus.

   Philippians 4:19

Heavenly Father, I thank You and praise You for all the ways You have shown me mercy and grace, and I ask for the blessing of Your presence throughout this day. I know that I could not get through this time of stress without Your outpouring of grace. Give me reminders today of Your goodness. Amen

Change is frightening. Whether you are mourning the loss of a loved one, preparing to leave a home you love, searching for a job, or even just finding yourself in a new stage of life, change can bring about high levels of stress. It may feel like if you can just move fast enough, and just do enough, you can control the change. But this is impossible on your own. No matter what that change is, the presence of God goes before you preparing the way. Have confidence that on the other side of this change, no matter what the new world looks like, God will be there.

*There is an occasion for everything, and a time for
every activity under heaven*
    Ecclesiastes 3:1

———

*"Do not remember the past events, pay no attention
to things of old. Look, I am about to do something
new; even now it is coming. Do you not see it?
Indeed, I will make a way in the wilderness, rivers
in the desert."*
    Isaiah 43:18–19

———

*"Because I, the LORD, have not changed, you
descendants of Jacob have not been destroyed."*
    Malachi 3:6

Therefore, if anyone is in Christ, he is a new creation; the old has passed away, and see, the new has come!
    2 Corinthians 5:17

———

Jesus Christ is the same yesterday, today, and forever.
    Hebrews 13:8

Lord Jesus, I do not know what the future holds for me, and it fills me with fear. I know that this stress is not the end of my story, and that You have a far greater plan ahead of me, but right now it is impossible for me to see. No matter what the future brings, may I take heart that You are with me until the end of the age. Bring me peace in the midst of this change, that I may not fear what is to come. Amen

None of us are immune from hardships, loss, and grief; but we can take heart that no matter what has happened, the Lord promises to comfort us. Sometimes He comforts us directly, sometimes through circumstances, and sometimes through the people He places in our lives. Think about the ways that God has comforted you in your times of need.

Even when I go through the darkest valley, I fear no danger, for you are with me; your rod and your staff—they comfort me.

Psalm 23:4

————

Remember your word to your servant; you have given me hope through it. This is my comfort in my affliction: Your promise has given me life.

Psalm 119:49–50

————

As a mother comforts her son, so I will comfort you, and you will be comforted in Jerusalem.

Isaiah 66:13

Blessed are those who mourn, for they will be comforted.

Matthew 5:4

———

Blessed be the God and Father of our Lord Jesus Christ, the Father of mercies and the God of all comfort. He comforts us in all our affliction, so that we may be able to comfort those who are in any kind of affliction, through the comfort we ourselves receive from God.

2 Corinthians 1:3–4

Dear God, thank You for comforting me and healing my heart in times of trial. I am lost in my schedule and I know that the only way out is with Your guiding hand. Thank You for putting people in my life who bring me comfort and peace. Guide me to those whom You have chosen for me as kindred spirits. Guide my actions that I may be a source of comfort for others. Use my life as a blessing. Amen

The Lord commands us to love our neighbors as ourselves and to also love our enemies—godly compassion is speaking and acting out of love in the best interests of others. Just like you would be willing to drop everything to help your dearest friend, you should be just as willing to have compassion for a stranger. This level of compassion is not possible on your own, and is only possible through the Holy Spirit inside of you. Leave margin in your schedule for the Holy Spirit to give you opportunities to show compassion.

Yet he was compassionate; he atoned for their iniquity and did not destroy them. He often turned his anger aside and did not unleash all his wrath.

Psalm 78:38

———

When he went ashore, he saw a large crowd and had compassion on them, because they were like sheep without a shepherd. Then he began to teach them many things.

Mark 6:34

Carry one another's burdens; in this way you will fulfill the law of Christ.
     Galatians 6:2

———

And be kind and compassionate to one another, forgiving one another, just as God also forgave you in Christ.
     Ephesians 4:32

Lord, may Your Holy Spirit fill my heart and soul with concern for my family, friends, neighbors, colleagues, and even enemies. Father, sometimes it is difficult for me to have compassion on those I consider deserving of their grief. Remove this hate from within me. Help me to see people the way you see them, and not through my own weaknesses. Open up my heart to the people around me that I may be a willing conduit of Your love. Amen

At home, at work, in friendships, in families, in life—contentment is hard! We are constantly looking around to see what could be better, what we are missing out on, or what we used to have. The quickest route to contentment is through gratitude and trust; gratitude to God for what He has provided you and trust that He will continue to give you everything you need. Recognize the goodness in your life. See the good, and trust that God never fails to provide for your needs.

*"So don't worry, saying, 'What will we eat?' or
'What will we drink?' or 'What will we wear?'
For the Gentiles eagerly seek all these things,
and your heavenly Father knows that you need
them. But seek first the kingdom of God and his
righteousness, and all these things will be provided
for you. Therefore don't worry about tomorrow,
because tomorrow will worry about itself. Each day
has enough trouble of its own."*

  Matthew 6:31–34

———

*But godliness with contentment is great gain. For
we brought nothing into the world, and we can take
nothing out. If we have food and clothing, we will
be content with these.*

  1 Timothy 6:6–8

He then told them, "Watch out and be on guard against all greed, because one's life is not in the abundance of his possessions."

Luke 12:15

———

I don't say this out of need, for I have learned to be content in whatever circumstances I find myself. I know both how to make do with little, and I know how to make do with a lot. In any and all circumstances I have learned the secret of being content—whether well fed or hungry, whether in abundance or in need.

Philippians 4:11–12

Heavenly Father, thank You for Your unfailing love and faithfulness. Father, when I am lost in discontentment, push me to see all that You have provided for me. Do not allow me to continue to be blind, but open my eyes to the goodness that surrounds me exactly where I am. Grow in me a godly contentment, never wishing I was anywhere but exactly where You have placed me. Amen

Having courage doesn't mean that you feel no fear; rather it means having a willingness and readiness to proceed despite the fear. It means working through your grief, knowing that even when you are at your worst, God is always at His best. Choose to have courage even when you are at the edge of breaking, trusting that God is enough and will pull you through.

"Haven't I commanded you: be strong and courageous? Do not be afraid or discouraged, for the LORD *your God is with you wherever you go."*
    Joshua 1:9

———

I always let the LORD *guide me. Because he is at my right hand, I will not be shaken.*
    Psalm 16:8

———

Wait for the LORD*; be strong, and let your heart be courageous. Wait for the* LORD*.*
    Psalm 27:14

Be alert, stand firm in the faith, be courageous, be strong.

1 Corinthians 16:13

———

For God has not given us a spirit of fear, but one of power, love, and sound judgment.

2 Timothy 1:7

Dear God, grant me a sense of Your strength and presence that I may face this day and its challenges with courage. Do not allow me to despair or cower. No matter the obstacle, You are enough; and I have courage, not because of anything that I am capable of, but because of the confidence that I have in You. Amen

When your heart is heavy and your mind is burdened, hold fast to the truth that God comforts us in all of our afflictions so that we may be able to comfort others with His love. On our darkest days, Christ is there to lift us up into the light. When you find yourself overwhelmed with the burdens of today, allow these verses to fill your heart and bring you back to the truth.

The LORD sits enthroned over the flood; the LORD sits enthroned, King forever. The LORD gives his people strength; the LORD blesses his people with peace.

    Psalm 29:10–11

———

The LORD is near the brokenhearted; he saves those crushed in spirit.

    Psalm 34:18

———

"Do not fear, for I am with you; do not be afraid, for I am your God. I will strengthen you; I will help you; I will hold on to you with my righteous right hand."

    Isaiah 41:10

Answer me quickly, LORD; my spirit fails.
Don't hide your face from me, or I will be like those
going down to the Pit.
Let me experience your faithful love in the morning,
for I trust in you. Reveal to me the way I should go
because I appeal to you.

    Psalm 143:7–8

———

I will give you the treasures of darkness and riches
from secret places, so that you may know that I am
the LORD. I am the God of Israel, who calls you by
your name.

    Isaiah 45:3

Dear Jesus, You were a man of sorrows and acquainted with a busy schedule—please fill my heart with Your strength and peace. Meet me where I am, and help me to find the way back into the light. My spirit is crushed, but I know You have saved me and will continue to do so. Be my strength when I am weak, my joy when I have none, and my light when I wander in darkness. Amen

More emails will come, more meetings will be scheduled, the kids will need new clothes, there will always be one more thing on your to-do list. This level of drive can push you to burn out, but it is not by your own strength that you meet success. If God's will is your ultimate goal, His strength will sustain you. Never tire of doing what is good.

The one who works his land will have plenty of food, but whoever chases fantasies lacks sense.
    Proverbs 12:11

———

The slacker craves, yet has nothing, but the diligent is fully satisfied.
    Proverbs 13:4

———

The plans of the diligent certainly lead to profit, but anyone who is reckless certainly becomes poor.
    Proverbs 21:5

Let us not get tired of doing good, for we will reap at the proper time if we don't give up.

Galatians 6:9

———

Whatever you do, do it from the heart, as something done for the Lord and not for people, knowing that you will receive the reward of an inheritance from the Lord. You serve the Lord Christ.

Colossians 3:23–24

Heavenly Father, I am worn out. My schedule is exhausting and overwhelming, and I cannot see the light at the end of the tunnel. Lord, I know that the work I am doing is ultimately for You, but I am running on fumes. Hold me fast to the task that You have called me to. Remind me daily to push diligently to the end, and run the race well. Amen

Sometimes the right and wrong answers are easy to see. Should I kill someone? No. Should I read my Bible? Yes. But other times the answers are not as clear. Should I complain to my friend about how difficult my day was? Where should I go to make new friends? Which church should I join? Luckily, these are not decisions you have to make on your own. The Holy Spirit is our ever-present Helper who grants us wisdom so that we can know and do the will of God in all situations.

So give your servant a receptive heart to judge your people and to discern between good and evil. For who is able to judge this great people of yours?
     1 Kings 3:9

———

Now if any of you lacks wisdom, he should ask God—who gives to all generously and ungrudgingly—and it will be given to him.
     James 1:5

———

Don't stifle the Spirit. Don't despise prophecies, but test all things. Hold on to what is good. Stay away from every kind of evil.
     1 Thessalonians 5:19–22

And I pray this: that your love will keep on growing in knowledge and every kind of discernment, so that you may approve the things that are superior and may be pure and blameless in the day of Christ.
   Philippians 1:9–10

———

Dear friends, do not believe every spirit, but test the spirits to see if they are from God, because many false prophets have gone out into the world.
   1 John 4:1

Holy Spirit, may my spirit be open and receptive to Your prompting and leading so that I discern what is right and good in all things. Let my discernment be so strong that I can hear You calling out the directions long before I am led astray. Place in me a heart that sees truth. Amen

Feeling busy can lead us into a feeling of dissatisfaction, either with our jobs, our families, or our lives overall. When you feel dissatisfied, it is often not because what you have is not enough, but because you have forgotten that only God can fully satisfy your soul. Rediscover the abundance around you by practicing gratitude and thanksgiving, even in the midst of chaos.

For he has satisfied the thirsty and filled the
hungry with good things.
    Psalm 107:9

———

You open your hand and satisfy the desire of every
living thing.
    Psalm 145:16

———

"I am the bread of life," Jesus told them. "No one
who comes to me will ever be hungry, and no one
who believes in me will ever be thirsty again."
    John 6:35

The LORD will always lead you, satisfy you in a parched land, and strengthen your bones.
You will be like a watered garden and like a spring whose water never runs dry.

    Isaiah 58:11

———

Now may the God of hope fill you with all joy and peace as you believe so that you may overflow with hope by the power of the Holy Spirit.

    Romans 15:13

Dear God, no good thing do You withhold from Your people. Help me see the goodness all around me and to delight in Your good and perfect gifts. Remind me daily that my satisfaction comes not from what I can complete, but from You, and You alone. Amen

God places people in our lives for a reason and for our good. Seek out those who bring you encouragement. Pray for those you can bring encouragement to. Never hold in kindness that can be spread to lift up those around you. Even when you are stressed beyond measure, look for opportunities in life to cheer others up. You never know when those words are God pouring out encouragement through you to others.

The LORD is the one who will go before you. He will be with you; he will not leave you or abandon you. Do not be afraid or discouraged.

    Deuteronomy 31:8

———

God is our refuge and strength, a helper who is always found in times of trouble.

    Psalm 46:1

———

"Aren't five sparrows sold for two pennies? Yet not one of them is forgotten in God's sight. Indeed, the hairs of your head are all counted. Don't be afraid; you are worth more than many sparrows."

    Luke 12:6–7

"I have told you these things so that in me you may have peace. You will have suffering in this world. Be courageous! I have conquered the world."

    John 16:33

———

And let us watch out for one another to provoke love and good works, not neglecting to gather together, as some are in the habit of doing, but encouraging each other, and all the more as you see the day approaching.

    Hebrews 10:24–25

Christ Jesus, may Your Spirit strengthen and encourage my heart today. Comfort me in my grief, and lift me out of my discouraged state. Show me those around me who need my encouragement. Place on my heart those friends who need a kind word today. Allow me to be the tool You use to help lift up everyone I meet today. Help me to push what is unimportant out of my schedule, so that I can find the time for the encouragement I so desperately need. Amen

Failure is part of life. It is not the failure in itself, but our ability to turn around and use that failure that sanctifies us. Unfortunately, it is too common for us to let our failures run our lives, to create unneeded stress remembering what happened last time. Though failures of any kind can crush our spirits, we have the assurance that God's purposes can never be thwarted. Walk in victory, knowing that any past failures are in the past, and God will use all to His glory.

He brought me up from a desolate pit, out of the muddy clay, and set my feet on a rock, making my steps secure. He put a new song in my mouth, a hymn of praise to our God. Many will see and fear, and they will trust in the Lord.

Psalm 40:2–3

———

Now we have this treasure in clay jars, so that this extraordinary power may be from God and not from us. We are afflicted in every way but not crushed; we are perplexed but not in despair; we are persecuted but not abandoned; we are struck down but not destroyed.

2 Corinthians 4:7–9

A person's steps are established by the LORD, and he takes pleasure in his way. Though he falls, he will not be overwhelmed, because the LORD supports him with his hand.

Psalm 37:23–24

———

Brothers and sisters, I do not consider myself to have taken hold of it. But one thing I do: Forgetting what is behind and reaching forward to what is ahead, I pursue as my goal the prize promised by God's heavenly call in Christ Jesus.

Philippians 3:13–14

Heavenly Father, grant me grace in times of failure and help me press forward as I fix my eyes on Jesus. Clear the failures from my mind, and do not allow them to cause me stress when I find myself in a similar situation. Thank You for the abundance of forgiveness You have poured over me. Amen

God's everlasting faithfulness to His people is a deep source of hope, as well as an inspiration for how we should conduct ourselves in our relationships. No matter what we do, where we are, or what we are going through, God is faithful. He is steady, constant, prepared, and will be the strength that you need. Put your trust in Him, and it will never be betrayed.

Because of the LORD's faithful love we do not perish,
for his mercies never end. They are new every
morning; great is your faithfulness!
    Lamentations 3:22–23

His master said to him, "Well done, good and
faithful servant! You were faithful over a few
things; I will put you in charge of many things.
Share your master's joy."
    Matthew 25:21

If we are faithless, he remains faithful, for he
cannot deny himself.
    2 Timothy 2:13

Whoever is faithful in very little is also faithful in much, and whoever is unrighteous in very little is also unrighteous in much. So if you have not been faithful with worldly wealth, who will trust you with what is genuine? And if you have not been faithful with what belongs to someone else, who will give you what is your own?

Luke 16:10–12

———

Let us hold on to the confession of our hope without wavering, since he who promised is faithful.

Hebrews 10:23

Dear God, Lamentations is the perfect example of a people lost. Right now I am lost in my own created chaos. I am crying out to You and feel completely alone with what I am going through. Plant in my heart the words of Lamentations 3:22–23. Remind me every morning of Your new mercies. I know that You are faithful; and no matter what this life throws at me, I will not perish under it because You are faithful. Amen

FEAR

Fear comes in many forms: fear of the unknown, of the impossible, of broken trust. Any of these fears can be all consuming. But we have an almighty God who loves us and cares for us at all times. We have a powerful God who is strong through all things. We have an omnipresent God who never leaves us alone and a God who is greater than any of our fears. With God on our side, there is nothing to fear, and nothing to stand in our way.

Haven't I commanded you: be strong and courageous? Do not be afraid or discouraged, for the LORD your God is with you wherever you go.

Joshua 1:9

———

When I am afraid, I will trust in you.

Psalm 56:3

———

You did not receive a spirit of slavery to fall back into fear. Instead, you received the Spirit of adoption, by whom we cry out, "Abba, Father!"

Romans 8:15

For God has not given us a spirit of fear, but one of power, love, and sound judgment.

    2 Timothy 1:7

———

Humble yourselves, therefore, under the mighty hand of God, so that he may exalt you at the proper time, casting all your cares on him, because he cares about you.

    1 Peter 5:6–7

Abba, Father, I cry out to You for Your protection and comfort. I'm overwhelmed with fear. Fear of the future and the unknown. I know that my fear stems from distrust, and that if I truly trusted You the way I say I do, then I would not have any fear. Thank You for Your faithful love and comfort. Continue to shelter me when I feel afraid. Amen

Constantly busy with work, children, school, and family obligations, fellowship with friends and fellow believers can be a difficult thing to find time for. When you do not intentionally schedule it into your week, it can become a thing of the past. But it is important to refresh your heart and soul. Find time this week to be around friends, not as an obligation or with any agenda, but just to fill your cup.

Iron sharpens iron, and one person sharpens another.

　　Proverbs 27:17

———

Two are better than one because they have a good reward for their efforts. For if either falls, his companion can lift him up; but pity the one who falls without another to lift him up.

　　Ecclesiastes 4:9–10

Carry one another's burdens; in this way you will fulfill the law of Christ.

Galatians 6:2

———

Therefore encourage one another and build each other up as you are already doing.

1 Thessalonians 5:11

———

And let us watch out for one another to provoke love and good works, not neglecting to gather together, as some are in the habit of doing, but encouraging each other, and all the more as you see the day approaching.

Hebrews 10:24–25

Dear Jesus, my heavenly Friend, please reveal to me ways I can spend more time in fellowship and build up others in my community. Show me the times in my schedule where I need to create margin to spend with the people who refresh my soul. Allow my presence to be a blessing to others. Amen

Forgiving someone who has hurt you means you no longer call to mind their fault or error—this extends grace to them and freedom for you. But it is not something that comes naturally or easily, especially when the hurt has been caused by someone you trusted. This level of forgiveness is only possible by leaning on the Holy Spirit within you and allowing Him to take control of cleaning your heart.

"*Therefore I tell you, her many sins have been forgiven; that's why she loved much. But the one who is forgiven little, loves little.*"
   Luke 7:47

———

Live in harmony with one another. Do not be proud; instead, associate with the humble. Do not be wise in your own estimation. Do not repay anyone evil for evil. Give careful thought to do what is honorable in everyone's eyes. If possible, as far as it depends on you, live at peace with everyone.
   Romans 12:16–18

*Be kind and compassionate to one another,
forgiving one another, just as God also forgave you
in Christ.*

> *Ephesians 4:32*

———

*As God's chosen ones, holy and dearly loved, put on
compassion, kindness, humility, gentleness, and
patience, bearing with one another and forgiving
one another if anyone has a grievance against
another. Just as the Lord has forgiven you, so you
are also to forgive.*

> *Colossians 3:12–13*

Dear God, it is easy for me to say that I forgive someone, but to actually release the resentment from my heart and let it be as if nothing ever happened . . . well I do not have any idea how to do that. Sometimes I feel trapped by the grudges and feelings of hurt that I have chosen to hold on to. I know that the feelings are not only damaging me, but my relationships as well. Please, just as You forgave all my debts and wrongs through Christ, empower me to extend forgiveness to those who have mistreated or hurt me. Amen

Friendship is not usually something that just knocks on your front door and stays forever. It needs to be invited, fostered, cared for, and encouraged. Precious are the friends, neighbors, and colleagues in our lives who faithfully stand by us through joys and sorrows, victories and failures, gains and loss. Find a way today to show the people in your life how much their friendship means to you.

Two are better than one because they have a good
reward for their efforts. For if either falls, his
companion can lift him up; but pity the one who
falls without another to lift him up.
　　Ecclesiastes 4:9–10

———

"No one has greater love than this: to lay down
his life for his friends. You are my friends if you
do what I command you. I do not call you servants
anymore, because a servant doesn't know what his
master is doing. I have called you friends, because
I have made known to you everything I have heard
from my Father."
　　John 15:13–15

Iron sharpens iron, and one person sharpens another.

>   *Proverbs 27:17*

———

Dear friends, let us love one another, because love is from God, and everyone who loves has been born of God and knows God.

>   *1 John 4:7*

———

Therefore encourage one another and build each other up as you are already doing.

>   *1 Thessalonians 5:11*

Lord Jesus, who called His disciples friends, thank You for demonstrating God's love for us and how best to love one another. Help me to be intentional in my relationships and to grow lifelong friendships. I thank You so much for the friends that You have placed in life, and I pray that You allow me to be a blessing to them as well. Amen

HUMILITY

There is a balance that many people find themselves in, trying to counter-balance their pride by putting themselves down. This is not the same as humility. The key to cultivating true humility isn't to act self-deprecating but to simply not think of oneself much at all. Recognize that it is not about us, but only about God. Give importance to others simply because they are God's creation and deserve to be treated as such.

Sitting down, he called the Twelve and said to them, "If anyone wants to be first, he must be last and servant of all."

Mark 9:35

————

Live in harmony with one another. Do not be proud; instead, associate with the humble. Do not be wise in your own estimation.

Romans 12:16

————

Do nothing out of selfish ambition or conceit, but in humility consider others as more important than yourselves.

Philippians 2:3

*Adopt the same attitude as that of Christ Jesus,
who, existing in the form of God, did not consider
equality with God as something to be exploited.
Instead he emptied himself by assuming the form
of a servant, taking on the likeness of humanity.
And when he had come as a man, he humbled
himself by becoming obedient to the point of
death—even to death on a cross.*

    Philippians 2:5–8

———

*Who among you is wise and understanding? By
his good conduct he should show that his works are
done in the gentleness that comes from wisdom.*

    James 3:13

Lord Jesus, who demonstrated perfect selflessness, please be my vision and my constant focus so that I forget myself completely. It is so easy for me to shift my focus onto myself, and even when I try to correct, I do so by putting myself down. Let me be so consumed by You, that there are no thoughts left for myself. Amen

Impulsive behavior is what flows out of your heart without thought or reflection. The feeling that most reliably follows an impulsive word or action is regret, because our hearts are full of sinful desires. Choose instead to be patient and deliberate. Fill yourself with wisdom, so that when an impulsive decision is needed, what flows out instinctively is God's Word and not your own.

Discretion will watch over you, and understanding will guard you. It will rescue you from the way of evil—from anyone who says perverse things.
    Proverbs 2:11–12

———

So if you have been raised with Christ, seek the things above, where Christ is, seated at the right hand of God. Set your minds on things above, not on earthly things.
    Colossians 3:1–2

For we all stumble in many ways. If anyone does not stumble in what he says, he is mature, able also to control the whole body.

  James 3:2

———

Watch yourselves so you don't lose what we have worked for, but that you may receive a full reward. Anyone who does not remain in Christ's teaching but goes beyond it does not have God. The one who remains in that teaching, this one has both the Father and the Son.

  2 John 8–9

Lord God, when I am living in the urgent, my heart turns back to my sinful ways. I do the things I don't want to do, and I don't do the things I want to do. Father, I need Your help to cut away my impulsive behavior. Fill me with Your wisdom, so that I am protected from my own sinful desires. Control my words and actions, that I may not sin against You. Amen

We have all seen a leader fall from the height of influence because of a secret, a double standard, or even a double life. But integrity is not something that is suddenly developed or that is only needed by people in positions of authority. Godly integrity is required of all Christians and dictates that you be consistent in your values, decisions, behaviors, and speech. You will stumble, you will fall, but you will always be helped back up by your heavenly Father.

The one who lives with integrity lives securely, but whoever perverts his ways will be found out.
    Proverbs 10:9

————

Better the poor person who lives with integrity than the rich one who distorts right and wrong.
    Proverbs 28:6

————

Indeed, we are giving careful thought to do what is right, not only before the Lord but also before people.
    2 Corinthians 8:21

Whatever you do, do it from the heart, as something done for the Lord and not for people, knowing that you will receive the reward of an inheritance from the Lord. You serve the Lord Christ.

Colossians 3:23–24

———

Yet do this with gentleness and respect, keeping a clear conscience, so that when you are accused, those who disparage your good conduct in Christ will be put to shame.

1 Peter 3:16

Lord, may Your Holy Spirit keep fierce watch over my heart so that I remain honest and incorruptible, for Your glory. Pour Your wisdom into my heart, that I may have the words to fight all forms of temptation. Direct my steps that I may follow Your path. I know I do not have the ability to stay faithful on my own, but with Your help, I will succeed. Amen

Even surrounded by people it is easy to feel alone. Thanks to social media, and the fast pace of modern life many of us are left feeling isolated— but thanks to God's faithful presence and our community of believers, we never have to be alone. Jesus will never leave you or cancel plans. He is always available for you when you need Him. When you are lost in your grief, Jesus is right next to you ready to sit with you, as long as you need, and pull you up when you are ready.

My presence will go with you, and I will give you rest.

 Exodus 33:14

———

The LORD is the one who will go before you. He will be with you; he will not leave you or abandon you. Do not be afraid or discouraged.

 Deuteronomy 31:8

———

God provides homes for those who are deserted. He leads out the prisoners to prosperity, but the rebellious live in a scorched land.

 Psalm 68:6

*He heals the brokenhearted and bandages their
wounds.*

    Psalm 147:3

———

*Blessed be the God and Father of our Lord Jesus
Christ, the Father of mercies and the God of all
comfort. He comforts us in all our affliction, so that
we may be able to comfort those who are in any
kind of affliction, through the comfort we ourselves
receive from God.*

    2 Corinthians 1:3–4

Father of mercies, please comfort me in these times of loneliness so that I may be a comfort to others. Remind me that even in my deepest despair, no matter where I am, You are with me. Thank You for being a constant reminder that I am never alone. Continue to hold me in Your arms, and help me to be a shoulder for others to help them know that I am here for them. Amen

Money is an essential and valuable tool, but too much trust in it or desire for it can quickly lead us away from what's most important. Are you busy because you are pursuing God's will for your life? Or is it something else that you are rapidly chasing after? Relinquish your search for what the earth considers success, and pursue the higher calling of Jesus Christ.

"*No one can serve two masters, since either he will hate one and love the other, or he will be devoted to one and despise the other. You cannot serve both God and money.*"

    Matthew 6:24

———

Pay your obligations to everyone: taxes to those you owe taxes, tolls to those you owe tolls, respect to those you owe respect, and honor to those you owe honor.

    Romans 13:7

For the love of money is a root of all kinds of evil,
and by craving it, some have wandered away from
the faith and pierced themselves with many griefs.

    1 Timothy 6:10

———

Instruct those who are rich in the present age not to
be arrogant or to set their hope on the uncertainty
of wealth, but on God, who richly provides us with
all things to enjoy.

    1 Timothy 6:17

———

Keep your life free from the love of money. Be
satisfied with what you have, for he himself has
said, "I will never leave you or abandon you."

    Hebrews 13:5

Heavenly Father, who richly provides us with so much abundance, please keep my heart free from covetousness and the love of money. I want to believe that my desires are only for Your will, but again and again I find myself back at the alter of finance. Lord, continue to remind me of my need for redemption. Help me to let go of the idol of financial stability that I have created, and replace it with faith that You will provide for all of my needs. Amen

While other people can only see our actions, God can look at our hearts and see the motives behind what we do. Rather than self-seeking or people-pleasing, we should endeavor to do all things through genuine love for God and others. But that can be harder than it sounds. Look at your full schedule and activities and examine your true motivations for each item. Are they ultimately for yourself, for others, or for God's glory? Use these verses to remind yourself of the importance of what is in your heart.

But the LORD said to Samuel, "Do not look at his appearance or his stature because I have rejected him. Humans do not see what the LORD sees, for humans see what is visible, but the LORD sees the heart."

　1 Samuel 16:7

———

All a person's ways seem right to him, but the LORD weighs hearts.

　Proverbs 21:2

———

For am I now trying to persuade people, or God? Or am I striving to please people? If I were still trying to please people, I would not be a servant of Christ.

　Galatians 1:10

Do nothing out of selfish ambition or conceit, but in humility consider others as more important than yourselves.

Philippians 2:3

———

Instead, just as we have been approved by God to be entrusted with the gospel, so we speak, not to please people, but rather God, who examines our hearts.

1 Thessalonians 2:4

Lord, please weigh my heart and my reasons for doing the things I do, and reveal to me any motives that don't glorify You. Help me to pull out those motives and change them. Give me a genuine love for the people around me, and move my heart to be so focused on You, that everything I do is glorifying to Your name. Amen

OBEDIENCE

Our first sinful instinct at birth is to rebel against obedience, to desire control. As we grow, this sinful desire only becomes more deeply rooted, unless we allow the Holy Spirit to tear it out of us. Obedience means yielding to the will of God, which is to love Him with all of your heart, soul, and mind, and to love your neighbor as yourself. Put Christ above all else and watch how your life is transformed.

I have chosen the way of truth; I have set your ordinances before me.
    Psalm 119:30

———

"If you love me, you will keep my commands."
    John 14:15

———

Peter and the apostles replied, "We must obey God rather than people."
    Acts 5:29

The one who keeps his commands remains in him, and he in him. And the way we know that he remains in us is from the Spirit he has given us.

1 John 3:24

———

For this is what love for God is: to keep his commands. And his commands are not a burden, because everyone who has been born of God conquers the world. This is the victory that has conquered the world: our faith.

1 John 5:3–4

Lord, may Your Spirit guide me in all my thoughts, words, and actions so that I am fully submitted to Your will. Tear out the sinful desires of my heart, and replace them with full humility and gracious understanding. I lay down my life at Your feet. Amen

The liveliness of children or the demands of the workplace can rattle your nerves, but take care to avoid making wrong choices or damaging your relationships. Remember the amount of patience that God has given you in your life, and pass it on to the people around you. Not one of us is perfect, and we all need grace and time to find the right path.

The end of a matter is better than its beginning;
a patient spirit is better than a proud spirit.
  Ecclesiastes 7:8

———

Now if we hope for what we do not see, we eagerly
wait for it with patience.
  Romans 8:25

———

My dear brothers and sisters, understand this:
Everyone should be quick to listen, slow to speak,
and slow to anger, for human anger does not
accomplish God's righteousness.
  James 1:19–20

*Therefore, brothers and sisters, be patient until
the Lord's coming. See how the farmer waits for
the precious fruit of the earth and is patient with
it until it receives the early and the late rains.
You also must be patient. Strengthen your hearts,
because the Lord's coming is near.*

    James 5:7–8

———

*The Lord does not delay his promise, as some
understand delay, but is patient with you, not
wanting any to perish but all to come to repentance.*

    2 Peter 3:9

Heavenly Father, You are patient and slow to anger—please help me be still and wait patiently for You. When I start to lose my way and my temper, give me Your calming touch, and help me to take a step back and remember what is really important. Thank You for the strength that You lend to me when I do not have enough myself. Amen

If you are at peace in all of your relationships, it is only a matter of time before conflict will arise. Rather than worry over what has happened in the past or what might happen in the future, be still with the Lord in the peace of the present moment. Be the one to ask for forgiveness, rather than holding on to resentment. Make the first step toward peace.

You will keep the mind that is dependent on you in perfect peace, for it is trusting in you.

   Isaiah 26:3

―――――

And the peace of God, which surpasses all understanding, will guard your hearts and minds in Christ Jesus. Finally brothers and sisters, whatever is true, whatever is honorable, whatever is just, whatever is pure, whatever is lovely, whatever is commendable—if there is any moral excellence and if there is anything praiseworthy—dwell on these things.

   Philippians 4:7–8

Peace I leave with you. My peace I give to you. I do not give to you as the world gives. Don't let your heart be troubled or fearful.

    John 14:27

———

For I am persuaded that neither death nor life, nor angels nor rulers, nor things present nor things to come, nor powers, nor height nor depth, nor any other created thing will be able to separate us from the love of God that is in Christ Jesus our Lord.

    Romans 8:38–39

Lord Jesus, I feel chaos and conflict in so many areas of my life. It is easy for me to be caught in the mess and forget the perfect peace that You have laid out for me. May Your perfect peace guard my heart and mind as I trust in You. Grant me the humility to seek out peace and be the one to lay down my pride at the feet of conflict, that my relationships may be redeemed. Amen

In the same way that our friendships and relationships with people need communication to be strengthened, so does our relationship with God. He has blessed us with the ability to speak to Him at all times, whenever we need Him. Especially when we are lost in busyness, the best gift is dedicated time with our Creator. No matter how we come to the Lord, whether to present our requests or to sit silently in His presence, we can trust that He hears us.

"Whenever you pray, you must not be like the hypocrites, because they love to pray standing in the synagogues and on the street corners to be seen by people. . . . But when you pray, go into your private room, shut your door, and pray to your Father who is in secret. And your Father who sees in secret will reward you. When you pray, don't babble like the Gentiles, since they imagine they'll be heard for their many words. . . .

"Therefore, you should pray like this: Our Father in heaven, your name be honored as holy. Your kingdom come. Your will be done on earth as it is in heaven. Give us today our daily bread. And forgive us our debts, as we also have forgiven our debtors. And do not bring us into temptation, but deliver us from the evil one.

"For if you forgive others their offenses, your heavenly Father will forgive you as well. But if you don't forgive others, your Father will not forgive your offenses."

Matthew 6:5–15

Pray constantly.

    1 Thessalonians 5:17

———

In the same way the Spirit also helps us in our weakness, because we do not know what to pray for as we should, but the Spirit himself intercedes for us with unspoken groanings.

    Romans 8:26

———

Don't worry about anything, but in everything, through prayer and petition with thanksgiving, present your requests to God.

    Philippians 4:6

Lord Jesus, just as You taught Your followers how to pray, instill in me a deep desire to seek Your presence. Send reminders into my life of my need to spend time with You. Help me to remember to not only speak in my prayers, but to sit and listen to what You have to say to me. Give me rest in Your presence, that my spirit may be healed. Amen

Pride comes in many shapes and sizes.
Arrogance tells us we are better than others,
low self-esteem tells us we are worse, and
praise makes us feel important, but they are all
signs of pride, because they all put the focus
on ourselves. Though we may be blessed with
wisdom, success, and happy relationships, we
can avoid pride by remembering that all good
things are ours by the grace of God.

When arrogance comes, disgrace follows, but with humility comes wisdom.

    Proverbs 11:2

———

Everyone with a proud heart is detestable to the LORD; be assured, he will not go unpunished.

    Proverbs 16:5

———

A person's pride will humble him, but a humble spirit will gain honor.

    Proverbs 29:23

Live in harmony with one another. Do not be proud; instead, associate with the humble. Do not be wise in your own estimation.

    Romans 12:16

———

For if anyone considers himself to be something when he is nothing, he deceives himself.

    Galatians 6:3

Father God, please forgive the ways I puff myself up rather than humble myself under Your loving hand. Help me to forget about myself, and keep my eyes on You. When I fall into a trap of pride, pull me to repentance, that I may not continue to sin against You. I know that any good I am capable of is only because of You. Amen

Relationships can only stand the test of time if both people can be relied upon. A friend who lets you down will not be considered a close friend for very long. But being reliable is not as easy as it sounds, especially when you are overwhelmed with your own schedule. The best way is to stay consistent with your word; and when you fail (because you will fail), repent of your wrong doing, and ask for forgiveness.

He will not allow your foot to slip; your Protector will not slumber.

Psalm 121:3

————

"But let your 'yes' mean 'yes,' and your 'no' mean 'no.' Anything more than this is from the evil one."

Matthew 5:37

Whoever is faithful in very little is also faithful in much, and whoever is unrighteous in very little is also unrighteous in much.

Luke 16:10

———

What you have heard from me in the presence of many witnesses, commit to faithful men who will be able to teach others also.

2 Timothy 2:2

Father, help me to stop making false promises where I cannot follow through. I want to be a reliable friend, but I know that I cannot do that on my own. I need Your strength. Thank You for being my example of what it means to be reliable. You are always there for me, and I know that with Your power behind me, I will be able to be reliable. Amen

Chronic stress is quickly becoming a national crisis that threatens our health—but God is our ever-present helper in times of trouble. Lay your burdens at His feet, and do not allow yourself to become overwhelmed with the temporary problems of this world. Cast your burdens on Him, and He will carry you through this time of stress.

Cast your burden on the LORD, and he will sustain you; he will never allow the righteous to be shaken.
   Psalm 55:22

———

Commit your activities to the LORD, and your plans will be established.
   Proverbs 16:3

———

"For I am the LORD your God, who holds your right hand, who says to you, 'Do not fear, I will help you.'"
   Isaiah 41:13

"*Come to me, all of you who are weary and burdened, and I will give you rest. Take up my yoke and learn from me, because I am lowly and humble in heart, and you will find rest for your souls. For my yoke is easy and my burden is light.*"

    Matthew 11:28–30

———

I am able to do all things through him who strengthens me.

    Philippians 4:13

Dear God, please fill me and strengthen me with Your Spirit when I feel overwhelmed, exhausted, and uncertain. Give me peace during the stress. Remind me daily of what You have trusted me to handle, and what I need to lay down at Your feet. Help me to trust You and to know that nothing I do can ever get in the way of Your plan. Amen

Your heart will dictate your definition of success. If success looks like a mansion with a nice car, your heart maybe filled with a greater desire for money than you realized. Being a Christian is not about being unsuccessful; it is turning away from the world's definition of success and working towards God's definition. Whether you succeed or fail, your true identity is your relationship with the Lord Jesus, and if you are working toward God's ends, you will never fail.

Take delight in the LORD, and he will give you your heart's desires.

    Psalm 37:4

———

Commit your activities to the LORD, and your plans will be established.

    Proverbs 16:3

"For what will it benefit someone if he gains the whole world yet loses his life? Or what will anyone give in exchange for his life? For the Son of Man is going to come with his angels in the glory of his Father, and then he will reward each according to what he has done."

   Matthew 16:26–27

———

Humble yourselves before the Lord, and he will exalt you.

   James 4:10

Lord Jesus, the world has defined success through material possessions and worldly fame, but I know that You have planned so much more for me. Father, help me to see success through Your eyes. May I value new brothers and sisters in the kingdom more than any amount of gold. May I see the success of the Church on the earth as the ultimate goal. Amen

VERSE INDEX